The Nation's #1 Educational

The **McGraw·Hill** Companies

The McGraw·Hill JUNIOR ACADEMIC™ SERIES

Preschool

Sound Patterns

Consonants • Letters & Sounds

A McGraw·Hill/Warner Bros. Workbook

Table of Contents

Beginning Sound D 3

Beginning Sound D 4

Final Sound D 5

Beginning Sound M 6

Beginning Sound M 7

Final Sound M 8

Beginning Sound S 9

Beginning Sound S 10

Final Sound S 11

Review 12

Review 13

Beginning Sound B 14

Beginning Sound B 15

Final Sound B 16

Beginning Sound G 17

Beginning Sound G 18

Final Sound G 19

Beginning Sound G 20

Beginning Sound T 21

Beginning Sound T 22

Final Sound T 23

Review 24

Review 25

Beginning Sound F 26

Beginning Sound F 27

Final Sound F 28

Beginning Sound F 29

Beginning Sound L 30

Beginning Sound L 31

Final Sound L 32

Beginning Sound L 33

Beginning Sound N 34

Beginning Sound N 35

Final Sound N 36

Beginning Sound N 37

Review 38

Table of Contents (continued)

Review 39

Review 40

Review 41

Review 42

Review 43

Beginning Sound K 44

Final Sound K 45

Beginning Sound P 46

Final Sound P 47

Beginning Sound R 48

Final Sound R 49

Beginning Sound H 50

Beginning Sound J 51

Beginning Sound W 52

Review 53

Review 54

Beginning Sound C 55

Beginning Sound V 56

Beginning Sound Y 57

Beginning Sound Qu 58

Beginning Sound Z 59

Final Sound X 60

Review 61

Review 62

Review 63

Review 64

Answer Key 65

Credits:
McGraw-Hill Learning Materials Editorial/Production Team
Vincent F. Douglas, B.S. and M. Ed.
Tracy R. Paulus
Jennifer P. Blashkiw

Design Studio
Mike Legendre; Creativity On Demand

Warner Bros. Worldwide Publishing Editorial/ProductionTeam
Michael Harkavy   Charles Carney
Paula Allen   Allen Helbig
Victoria Selover

Illustrators
Cover: Renegade Animation
Interior: Ryan Dunlavey; SI International—Thompson Bros.

McGraw-Hill
Consumer Products

A Division of The McGraw·Hill Companies

Send all inquiries to:
McGraw-Hill Consumer Products
250 Old Wilson Bridge Road
Worthington, Ohio 43085

1-57768-239-4

BEGINNING SOUND D

Dd

Daffy Duck's Donut Dinner

Directions: Have your child look at the picture and say *Daffy Duck's Donut Dinner* while listening for the beginning d sound. Ask your child to name the items in the picture, then circle those that begin with the same d sound. **Skill:** Identifying the beginning sound d.

3

BEGINNING SOUND D

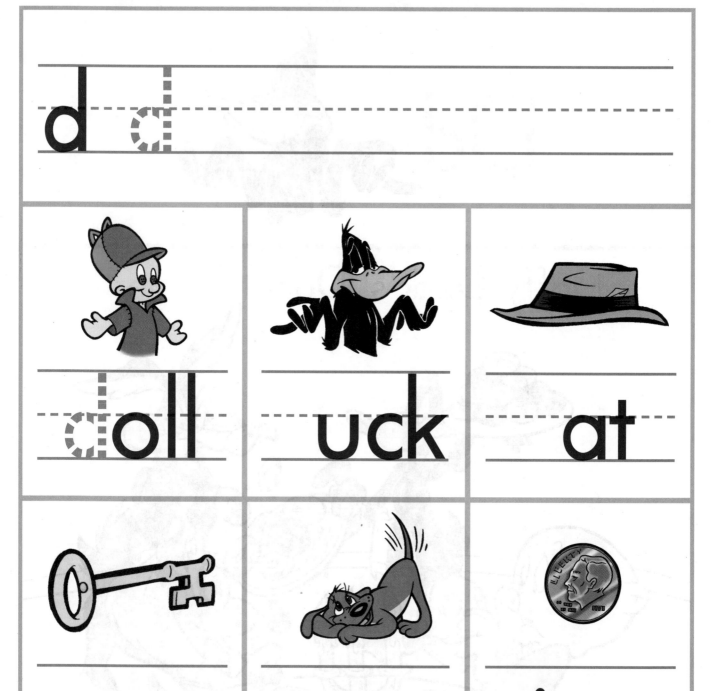

d d

doll uck at

ey og ime

4

FINAL SOUND D

d d

bed

li

cu

sle

Directions: Have your child trace and write *d* at the top of the page. Following the example, ask your child to name the pictures, then write *d* under those that end with the same sound as the first picture. **Skill:** Writing d; identifying the final sound d.

BEGINNING SOUND M

Mm

Marvin the Martian Meets Mice

MARTIAN MAGGOT

Directions: Have your child look at the picture and say *Marvin the Martian Meets Mice* while listening for the beginning m sound. Ask your child to name the items in the picture, then circle those that begin with the same m sound. **Skill:** Identifying the beginning sound m.

BEGINNING SOUND M

m m

 mop

ub

ask

 oon

ap

un

7

Directions: Have your child trace and write *m* at the top of the page. Following the example, ask your child to name the pictures, then write *m* under those that begin with the same sound as the first picture. **Skill:** Writing m; identifying the beginning sound m.

FINAL SOUND M

m m ----------------------------------

drum

ha _____

ru _____

cla _____

Directions: Have your child trace and write *m* at the top of the page. Following the example, ask your child
to name the pictures, then write *m* under those that end with the same sound as the first picture.
Skill: Writing m; identifying the final sound m.

BEGINNING SOUND S

Ss

Sylvester and his Son in a Sailboat

Directions: Have your child look at the picture and say *Sylvester and his Son in a Sailboat* while listening for the beginning s sound. Ask your child to name the items in the picture, then circle those that begin with the same s sound. **Skill:** Identifying the beginning sound s.

BEGINNING SOUND S

S s S

 six

 at

 un

 up

 alt

 ink

Directions: Have your child trace and write s at the top of the page. Following the example, ask your child to name the pictures, then write s under those that begin with the same sound as the first picture. **Skill:** Writing s; identifying the beginning sound s.

FINAL SOUND S

s S

bus

we

ga

plu

Directions: Have your child trace and write s at the top of the page. Following the example, ask your child to name the pictures, then write s under those that end with the same sound as the first picture. **Skill:** Writing s; identifying the final sound s.

d, m, s

REVIEW

RED = d   BLUE = m   YELLOW = s

Directions: Have your child name each character, then color the horse of the character whose name begins with *d* red, with *m* blue, with *s* yellow. **Skill:** Reviewing the beginning sounds d, m and s.

REVIEW

d m s

d m s

d m s

d m s

d m s

d m s

Directions: Have your child name each picture, then circle the letter that stands for the final sound. Ask your child to write the letter in the space provided. *Skill:* Reviewing the final sounds d, m, and s.

13

Bb

Bugs Bunny's Baseball Buddy

14

Directions: Have your child look at the picture and say *Bugs Bunny's Baseball Buddy* while listening for the beginning b sound. Ask your child to name the items in the picture, then circle those that begin with the same b sound. **Skill:** Identifying the beginning sound b.

BEGINNING SOUND B

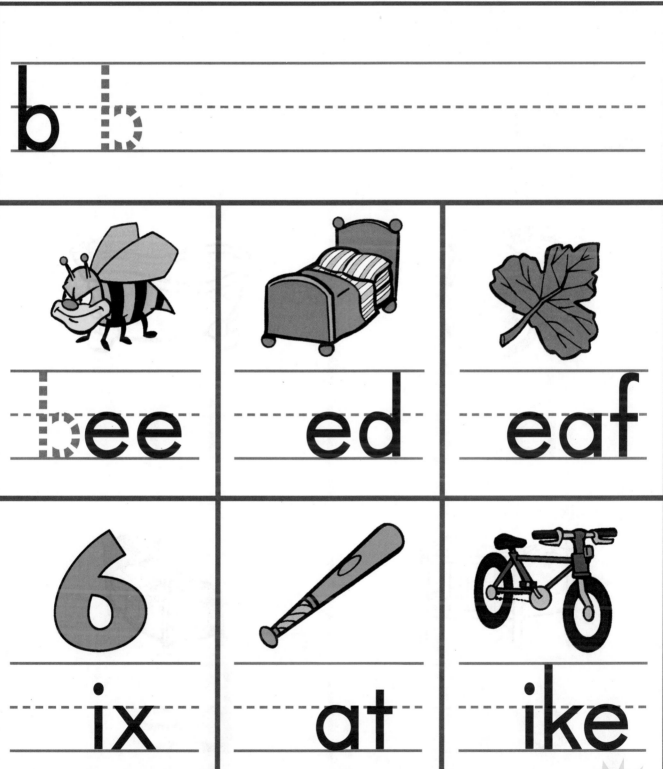

b   b

bee   ed   eaf

ix   at   ike

Directions: Have your child trace and write *b* at the top of the page. Following the example, ask your child to name the pictures, then write *b* under those that begin with the same sound as the first picture. **Skill:** Writing b; identifying the beginning sound b.

FINAL SOUND B

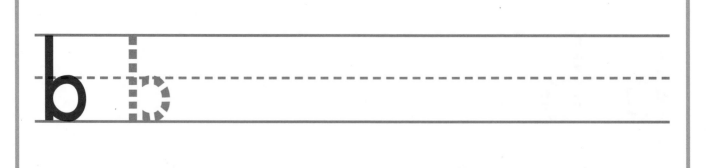

b | b

bib

tu

cri

be

Directions: Have your child trace and write *b* at the top of the page. Following the example, ask your child to name the pictures, then write *b* under those that end with the same sound as the first picture.
Skill: Writing b; identifying the final sound b.

BEGINNING SOUND G

Granny's Garden Gate

Directions: Have your child look at the picture and say *Granny's Garden Gate* while listening for the beginning g sound. Ask your child to name the items in the picture, then circle those that begin with the same g sound. **Skill:** Identifying the beginning sound g.

BEGINNING SOUND G

g g _____

gate

ey

olf

irl

ift

og

Directions: Have your child trace and write *g* at the top of the page. Following the example, ask your child to name the pictures, then write *g* under those that begin with the same sound as the first picture.
Skill: Writing g; identifying the beginning sound g.

 NAME _____

FINAL SOUND G

g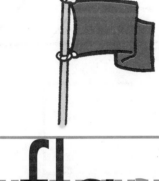

fla**g**

do

wi

pi

Directions: Have your child trace and write *g* at the top of the page. Following the example, ask your child to name the pictures, then write *g* under those that end with the same sound as the first picture.
Skill: Writing *g*; identifying the final sound *g*.

 19

BEGINNING SOUND G

Directions: Have your child name the pictures, then draw a line from each picture to a square in the gift box if the picture name begins with g. **Skill:** Identifying the beginning sound g.

BEGINNING SOUND T

T t

Tweety's Tiny Tent

Directions: Have your child look at the picture and say *Tweety's Tiny Tent* while listening for the beginning t sound. Ask your child to name the items in the picture, then circle those that begin with the same t sound. **Skill:** Identifying the beginning sound t.

21

BEGINNING SOUND T

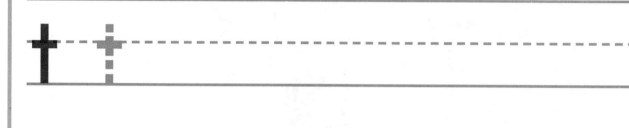

t t

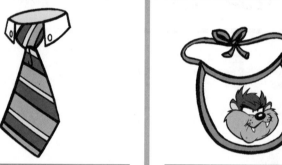

tie

ib

ive

ack

10

en

ire

22 👉

Directions: Have your child trace and write *t* at the top of the page. Following the example, ask your child to name the pictures, then write *t* under those that begin with the same sound as the first picture. **Skill:** Writing *t*; identifying the beginning sound *t*.

NAME

FINAL SOUND T

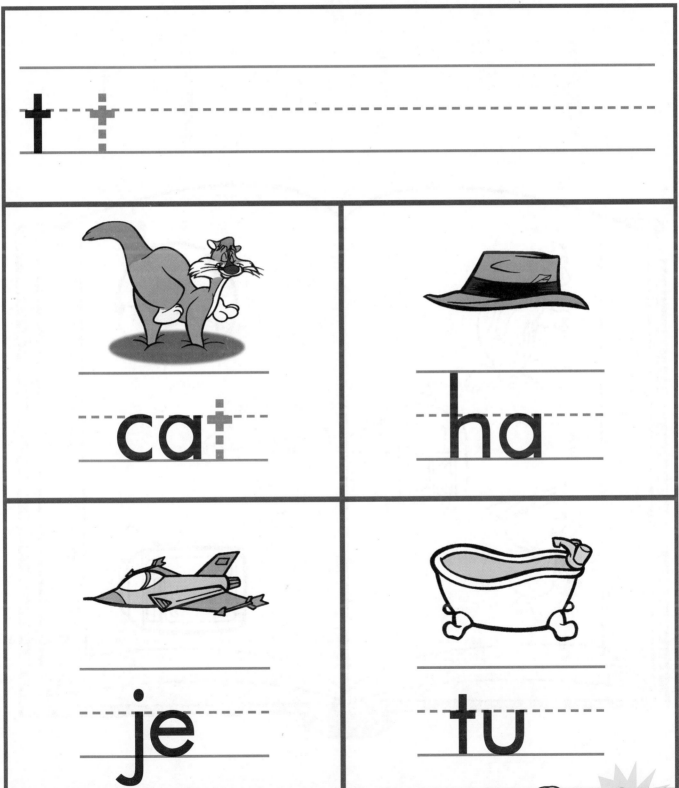

t

cat

ha

je

tu

Directions: Have your child trace and write *t* at the top of the page. Following the example, ask your child to name the pictures, then write *t* under those that end with the same sound as the first picture.
Skill: Writing t; identifying the final sound t.

 23

b, g, t

REVIEW

GREEN = b   RED = g   BLUE = t

Directions: Have your child name each picture, then color the pictures that begin with *b* green, with *g* red, and with *t* blue. **Skill:** Reviewing the beginning sounds b, g and t.

REVIEW

b, g, t

b g t

_____

- - - - - -

_____

b g t

_____

- - - - - -

_____

b g t

_____

- - - - - -

_____

b g t

_____

- - - - - -

_____

b g t

_____

- - - - - -

_____

b g t

_____

- - - - - -

_____

Directions: Have your child name each picture, then circle the letter that stands for the final sound. Ask your child to write the letter in the space provided. **Skill:** Reviewing the final sounds b, g, and t.

BEGINNING SOUND F

Ff

Foghorn's Fork Fell in the Fountain

Directions: Have your child look at the picture and say *Foghorn's Fork Fell in the Fountain* while listening for the beginning f sound. Ask your child to name the items in the picture, then circle those that begin with the same f sound. **Skill:** Identifying the beginning sound f.

f f _____

f̲ire

___oon

5

___ive

___oor

___ork

___ox

Directions: Have your child trace and write *f* at the top of the page. Following the example, ask your child to name the pictures, then write *f* under those that begin with the same sound as the first picture.
Skill: Writing f; identifying the beginning sound f.

FINAL SOUND F

f

lea f

el

roo

ma

Directions: Have your child trace and write _f_ at the top of the page. Following the example, ask your child to name the pictures, then write _f_ under those that end with the same sound as the first picture.
Skill: Writing f; identifying the final sound f.

BEGINNING SOUND F

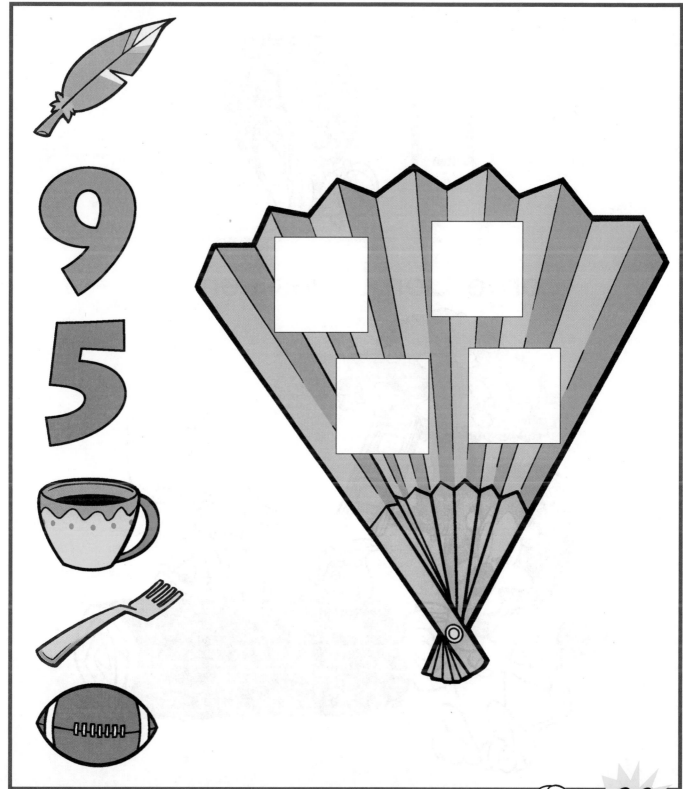

Directions: Have your child name the pictures, then draw a line from each picture to a square in the fan if the picture name begins with f. **Skill:** Identifying the beginning sound f.

29

BEGINNING SOUND L

L l

Large Lion Loves Lemons

30

Directions: Have your child look at the picture and say *Large Lion Loves Lemons* while listening for the beginning l sound. Ask your child to name the items in the picture, then circle those that begin with the same l sound. **Skill:** Identifying the beginning sound l.

BEGINNING SOUND L

l

| lips | ix | op |
| amp | ock | eaf |

Directions: Have your child trace and write *l* at the top of the page. Following the example, ask your child to name the pictures, then write *l* under those that begin with the same sound as the first picture.
Skill: Writing l; identifying the beginning sound l.

FINAL SOUND L

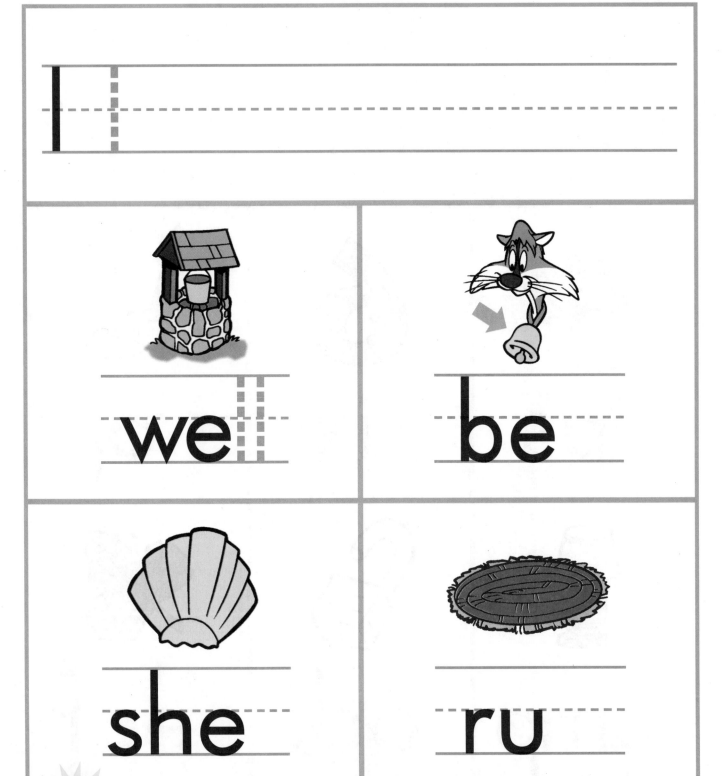

I

we**ll**

be__

she__

ru__

Directions: Have your child trace and write *l* at the top of the page. Following the example, ask your child to name the pictures, then write *ll* under those that end with the same sound as the first picture. **Skill:** Writing *l*; identifying the final sound *l*.

BEGINNING SOUND L

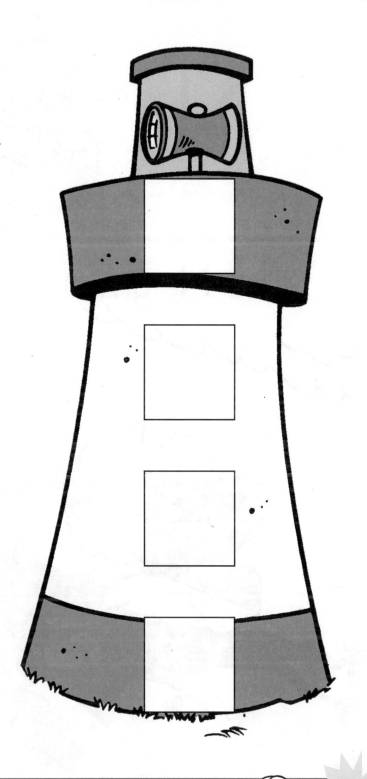

Directions: Have your child name the pictures, draw a line from each picture to a square in the lighthouse if the picture name begins with *l*. **Skill:** Identifying the beginning sound l.

BEGINNING SOUND N

Nn

The Neighbor in the Nest

34

Directions: Have your child look at the picture and say *The Neighbor in the Nest* while listening for the beginning n sound. Ask your child to name the items in the picture, then circle those that begin with the same n sound. **Skill:** Identifying the beginning sound n.

BEGINNING SOUND N

n n

nose

__et

__an

__ut

__ail

__aw

Directions: Have your child trace and write *n* at the top of the page. Following the example, ask your child to name the pictures, then write *n* under those that begin with the same sound as the first picture.
Skill: Writing n; identifying the beginning sound n.

 35

FINAL SOUND N

n n

sun

te

bi

pi

Directions: Have your child trace and write *n* at the top of the page. Following the example, ask your child to name the pictures, then write *n* under those that end with the same sound as the first picture.
Skill: Writing n; identifying the final sound n.

BEGINNING SOUND N

Directions: Have your child name the pictures, then draw a line from each picture to a square in the nest if the picture name begins with *n*. **Skill:** Identifying the beginning sound n.

37

REVIEW

f, l, n

RED | = f   ORANGE | = l   YELLOW | = n

4

9

Directions: Have your child name each charm on the necklace, then color the objects that begin with *f* red, with *l* orange, and with *n* yellow. **Skill:** Reviewing the beginning sounds f, l, and n.

f l n

f l n

f l n

f l n

f l n

f l n

Directions: Have your child name each picture, then circle the letter that stands for the final sound. Ask your child to write the letter in the space provided. **Skill:** Reviewing the final sounds f, l, and n.

39

REVIEW

Beginning Sounds

Directions: Have your child name the picture at the beginning of each row. Then ask your child to circle each picture in the row whose name begins with the same sound as the first picture. **Skill:** Reviewing beginning consonant sounds.

REVIEW

Beginning Sounds

Directions: Have your child name the picture at the beginning of each row. Then ask your child to circle each picture in the row whose name begins with the same sound as the first picture. **Skill:** Reviewing beginning consonant sounds.

41

REVIEW

Beginning
Sounds

_____
- - - - - - -
_____

_____
- - - - - - -
_____

_____
- - - - - - -
_____

_____
- - - - - - -
_____

_____
- - - - - - -
_____

_____
- - - - - - -
_____

_____
- - - - - - -
_____

_____
- - - - - - -
_____

_____
- - - - - - -
_____

Directions: Have your child name each picture, then write the letter that stands for the beginning sound.
Skill: Reviewing beginning consonant sounds.

REVIEW

Directions: Have your child name the pictures, then write the letter that stands for the final sound.
Skill: Reviewing final consonant sounds.

BEGINNING SOUND K

k k

kick

aby

iss

ettle

ey

an

Directions: Have your child trace and write k at the top of the page. Following the example, ask your child to name the pictures, then write k under those that begin with the same sound as the first picture.
Skill: Writing k; identifying the beginning sound k.

FINAL SOUND K

k k

hook   boo

rin   snea

Directions: Have your child trace and write *k* at the top of the page. Following the example, ask your child to name the pictures, then write *k* under those that end with the same sound as the first picture.
Skill: Writing k; identifying the final sound k.

BEGINNING SOUND P

p p

pie

able

ony

ear

adio

ail

46

Directions: Have your child trace and write p at the top of the page. Following the example, ask your child to name the pictures, then write p under those that begin with the same sound as the first picture.
Skill: Writing p; identifying the beginning sound p.

FINAL SOUND P

p p -

mop

lam - - - -

ma - - - -

ca - - - -

Directions: Have your child trace and write p at the top of the page. Following the example, ask your child to name the pictures, then write p under those that end with the same sound as the first picture.
Skill: Writing p; identifying the final sound p.

BEGINNING SOUND R

r r _____

r ug

ain

ite

ose

adio

oat

Directions: Have your child trace and write *r* at the top of the page. Following the example, ask your child to name the pictures, then write *r* under those that begin with the same sound as the first picture. **Skill:** Writing r; identifying the beginning sound r.

FINAL SOUND R

r  r

star

boo

4

fou

ca

Directions: Have your child trace and write *r* at the top of the page. Following the example, ask your child to name the pictures, then write *r* under those that end with the same sound as the first picture.
Skill: Writing r; identifying the final sound r.

BEGINNING SOUND H

h h ⌐

hand

en

orse

eart

ear

orn

Directions: Have your child trace and write *h* at the top of the page. Following the example, ask your child to name the pictures, then write *h* under those that begin with the same sound as the first picture.
Skill: Writing *h*; identifying the beginning sound h.

j j

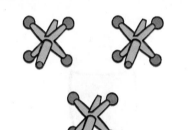

jacks

ar

ump

amp

udge

ug

Directions: Have your child trace and write *j* at the top of the page. Following the example, ask your child to name the pictures, then write *j* under those that begin with the same sound as the first picture.
Skill: Writing *j*; identifying the beginning sound *j*.

BEGINNING SOUND W

W W

web

ose

ug

ing

atch

ig

Directions: Have your child trace and write w at the top of the page. Following the example, ask your child to name the pictures, then write w under those that begin with the same sound as the first picture.
Skill: Writing w; identifying the beginning sound w.

Review

h, j, w

Directions: Have your child name the pictures in each box to find the two with the same beginning sound. Ask your child to circle the two pictures, then write the letter that stands for the beginning sound.
Skill: Reviewing the beginning sounds h, j and w.

REVIEW

Beginning Sounds

Directions: Have your child name each picture, then write the letter that stands for the beginning sound.
Skill: Reviewing beginning consonant sounds.

Claude Cat

c c _ _ _ _ _ _ _ _ _

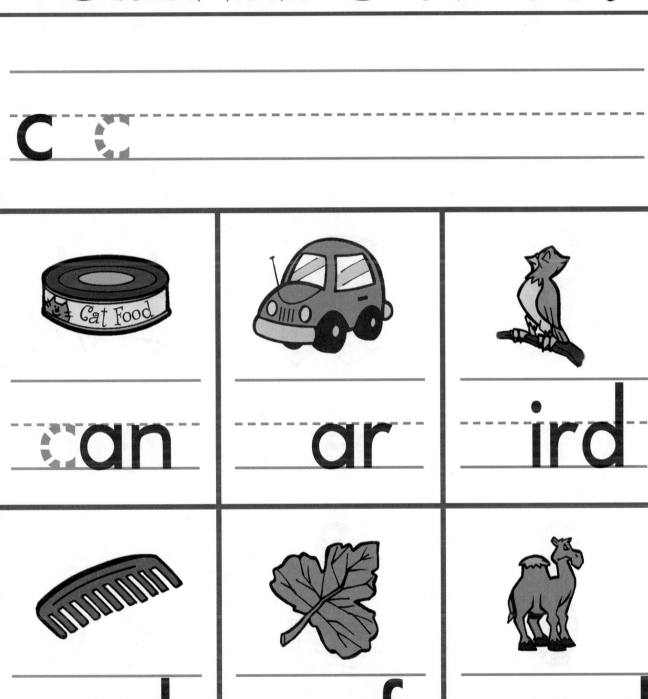

can

ar

ird

omb

eaf

amel

Directions: Have your child trace and write *c* at the top of the page. Following the example, ask your child to name the pictures, then write *c* under those that begin with the same sound as the first picture.
Skill: Writing *c*; identifying the beginning sound *c*.

BEGINNING SOUND V

V V

vine

est

ent

ase

et

ite

Directions: Have your child trace and write v at the top of the page. Following the example, ask your child to name the pictures, then write v under those that begin with the same sound as the first picture.

Skill: Writing v; identifying the beginning sound v.

BEGINNING SOUND Y

y y

yawn

uck

ak

ip

oose

es

Directions: Have your child trace and write y at the top of the page. Following the example, ask your child to name the pictures, then write y under those that begin with the same sound as the first picture.
Skill: Writing y; identifying the beginning sound y.

 57

BEGINNING SOUND Qu

qu qu

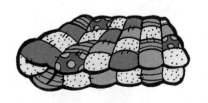

qu ilt

iet

eal

art

ack

ail

Directions: Have your child trace and write *qu* at the top of the page. Following the example, ask your child to name the pictures, then write *qu* under those that begin with the same sound as the first picture. **Skill:** Writing qu; identifying the beginning sound qu.

BEGINNING SOUND Z

z z _____

O		
zero	oo	ook
ish	ip	art

Directions: Have your child trace and write z at the top of the page. Following the example, ask your child to name the pictures, then write z under those that begin with the same sound as the first picture.
Skill: Writing z; identifying the beginning sound z.

FINAL SOUND X

X X

fix

boo

wa

o

si

sta

Directions: Have your child trace and write x at the top of the page. Following the example, ask your child to name the pictures, then write x under those that end with the same sound as the first picture.
Skill: Writing x; identifying the final sound x.

REVIEW

Directions: In the top four boxes, have your child name the pictures, then write the letter(s) that stands for the beginning sound. In the bottom two boxes, ask your child to name the pictures, then write the letter that stands for the final sound. **Skill:** Reviewing beginning and final consonant sounds.

REVIEW

Beginning Sounds

Directions: Have your child name the picture at the beginning of each row. Then ask your child to circle each picture in the row whose name begins with the same sound as the first picture.

Skill: Reviewing beginning consonant sounds.

REVIEW

Directions: Have your child name the picture at the beginning of each row. Then ask your child to circle each picture in the row whose name begins with the same sound as the first picture. *Skill:* Reviewing beginning consonant sounds.

REVIEW

Directions: Have your child name the picture at the beginning of each row. Then ask your child to circle each picture in the row whose name ends with the same sound as the first picture.

Skill: Reviewing final consonant sounds.

ANSWER KEY

BEGINNING SOUND D

Dd

Daffy Duck's Donut Dinner

Daffy Duck
dish
donuts

Directions: Have your child look at the picture and say *Daffy Duck's Donut Dinner* while listening for the beginning d sound. Ask your child to name the items in the picture, then circle those that begin with the same d sound. **Skill:** Identifying the beginning sound d.

3

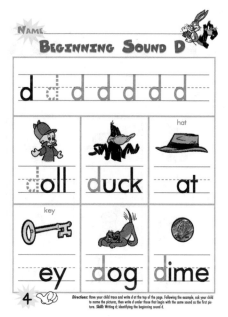

BEGINNING SOUND D

d d d d d d d

doll | duck | hat / at
key / ey | dog | dime

Directions: Have your child trace and write d at the top of the page. Following the example, ask your child to name the pictures, then write d under those that begin with the same sound as the first picture. **Skill:** Writing d; identifying the beginning sound d.

4

FINAL SOUND D

d d d d d d d

bed | lid
cup / cu | sled

Directions: Have your child trace and write d at the top of the page. Following the example, ask your child to name the pictures, then write d under those that end with the same sound as the first picture. **Skill:** Writing d; identifying the final sound d.

5

BEGINNING SOUND M

Mm

Marvin the Martian Meets Mice

map
Marvin the
Martian
mittens
mop
mouse

MARTIAN MAGGOT

Directions: Have your child look at the picture and say *Marvin the Martian Meets Mice* while listening for the beginning m sound. Ask your child to name the items in the picture, then circle those that begin with the same m sound. **Skill:** Identifying the beginning sound m.

6

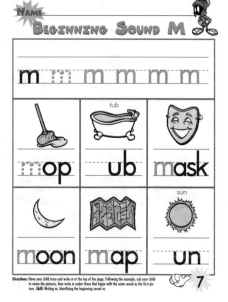

BEGINNING SOUND M

m m m m m m

mop | tub / ub | mask
moon | map | sun / un

Directions: Have your child trace and write m at the top of the page. Following the example, ask your child to name the pictures, then write m under those that begin with the same sound as the first picture. **Skill:** Writing m; identifying the beginning sound m.

7

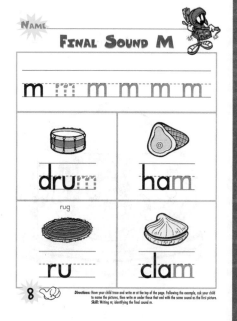

FINAL SOUND M

m m m m m m

drum | ham
rug / ru | clam

Directions: Have your child trace and write m at the top of the page. Following the example, ask your child to name the pictures, then write m under those that end with the same sound as the first picture. **Skill:** Writing m; identifying the final sound m.

8

ANSWER KEY

NAME

BEGINNING SOUND S

Ss

Sylvester and his Son in a Sailboat

sailboat
seal
submarine
sun
Sylvester Jr.
Sylvester

Directions: Have your child look at the picture and say *Sylvester and his Son in a Sailboat* while listening for the beginning s sound. Ask your child to name the items in the picture, then circle those that begin with the same s sound. **Skill:** Identifying the beginning sound s.

9

BEGINNING SOUND S

s S S S S S S

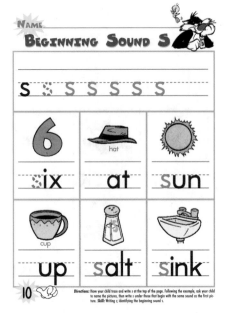

6	hat	sun
Six	at	sun
cup	salt	sink
up	salt	sink

10 **Directions:** Have your child trace and write s at the top of the page. Following the example, ask your child to name the pictures, then write s under those that begin with the same sound as the first picture. **Skill:** Writing s; identifying the beginning sound s.

FINAL SOUND S

s S S S S S S

	web
bus	we
gas	plus

Directions: Have your child trace and write s at the top of the page. Following the example, ask your child to name the pictures, then write s under those that end with the same sound as the first picture. **Skill:** Writing s; identifying the final sound s.

11

NAME

REVIEW

d, m, s

= d   = m   = s

12 **Directions:** Have your child name each character, then color the horse of the character whose name begins with d red, with m blue, with s yellow. **Skill:** Reviewing the beginning sounds d, m and s.

REVIEW

d, m, s

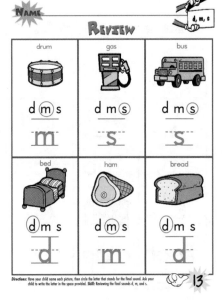

drum	gas	bus
d (m) s	d m (s)	d m (s)
m	s	s
bed	ham	bread
(d) m s	d (m) s	(d) m s
d	m	d

Directions: Have your child name each picture, then circle the letter that stands for the final sound. Ask your child to write the letter in the space provided. **Skill:** Reviewing the final sounds d, m, and s.

13

BEGINNING SOUND B

Bb

Bugs Bunny's Baseball Buddy

bag
baseball
basket
bat
Beaky
Buzzard
bench
bucket
Bugs
Bunny

14 **Directions:** Have your child look at the picture and say *Bugs Bunny's Baseball Buddy* while listening for the beginning b sound. Ask your child to name the items in the picture, then circle those that begin with the same b sound. **Skill:** Identifying the beginning sound b.

ANSWER KEY

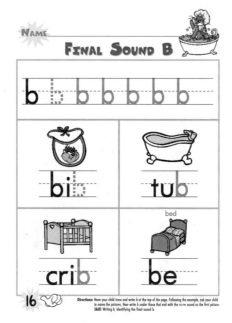

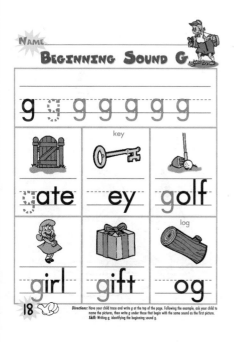

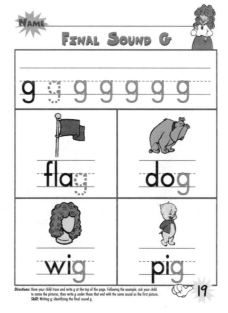

ANSWER KEY

Beginning Sound T

Tt

Tweety's Tiny Tent

table
television
tent
tree
Tweety

Directions: Have your child look at the picture and say *Tweety's Tiny Tent* while listening for the beginning t sound. Ask your child to name the items in the picture, then circle those that begin with the same t sound. *Skill:* Identifying the beginning sound t.

21

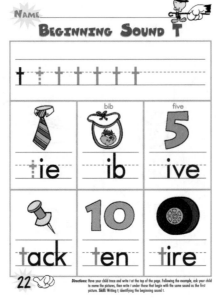

Beginning Sound T

t t t t t t t

	bib	five
tie	**t**ib	**t**ive
	10	
tack	**t**en	**t**ire

22

Directions: Have your child trace and write t at the top of the page. Following the example, ask your child to name the pictures, then write t under those that begin with the same sound as the first picture. *Skill:* Writing t; identifying the beginning sound t.

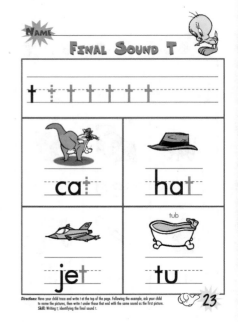

Final Sound T

t t t t t t t t

ca**t**	ha**t**
	tub
je**t**	tu**t**

Directions: Have your child trace and write t at the top of the page. Following the example, ask your child to name the pictures, then write t under those that end with the same sound as the first picture. *Skill:* Writing t; identifying the final sound t.

23

Review

= b	= g	= t

green
turtle
ball
red
gorilla
barn
red
girl
television
blue

24

Directions: Have your child name each picture, then color the pictures that begin with b green, with g red, and with t blue. *Skill:* Reviewing the beginning sounds b, g and t.

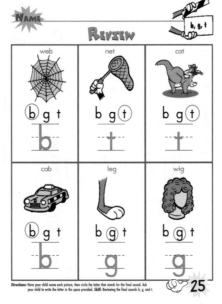

Review

web	net	cat
ⓑ g t	b ⓖ t	b g ⓣ
b	t	t
cab	leg	wig
ⓑ g t	b ⓖ t	b ⓖ t
b	g	g

Directions: Have your child name each picture, then circle the letter that stands for the final sound. Ask your child to write the letter in the space provided. *Skill:* Reviewing the final sounds b, g, and t.

25

Beginning Sound F

Ff

Foghorn's Fork Fell in the Fountain

fish
Foghorn
fork
fountain

26

Directions: Have your child look at the picture and say *Foghorn's Fork Fell in the Fountain* while listening for the beginning f sound. Ask your child to name the items in the picture, then circle those that begin with the same f sound. *Skill:* Identifying the beginning sound f.

ANSWER KEY

Beginning Sound F

f f f f f f f f

	moon	5
fire	**m**oon	**f**ive
door		
d**oor**	**fork**	**fox**

Directions: Have your child trace and write f at the top of the page. Following the example, ask your child to name the pictures, then write f under those that begin with the same sound as the first picture.
Skill: Writing f; identifying the beginning sound f.

27

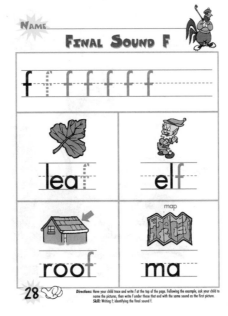

Final Sound F

f f f f f f f f

lea**f**	el**f**
	map
roo**f**	ma**p**

28

Directions: Have your child trace and write f at the top of the page. Following the example, ask your child to name the pictures, then write f under those that end with the same sound as the first picture.
Skill: Writing f; identifying the final sound f.

Beginning Sound F

feather
9 nine
5 five
cup
fork
football

Directions: Have your child name the pictures, then draw a line from each picture to a square in the fan if the picture name begins with f. **Skill:** Identifying the beginning sound f.

29

Beginning Sound L

L l

Large Lion Loves Lemons

ladder
lemon
lemonade
lion
log

30

Directions: Have your child look at the picture and say *Large Lion Loves Lemons* while listening for the beginning l sound. Ask your child to name the items in the picture, then circle those that begin with the same l sound. **Skill:** Identifying the beginning sound l.

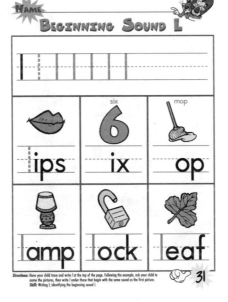

Beginning Sound L

	six	mop
lips	s**ix**	m**op**
lamp	**l**ock	**l**eaf

Directions: Have your child trace and write l at the top of the page. Following the example, ask your child to name the pictures, then write l under those that begin with the same sound as the first picture.
Skill: Writing l; identifying the beginning sound l.

31

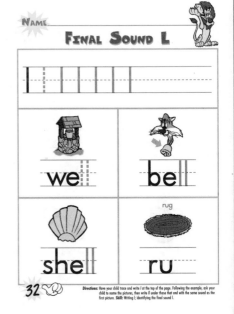

Final Sound L

wel**l**	bel**l**
	rug
shel**l**	ru**g**

32

Directions: Have your child trace and write l at the top of the page. Following the example, ask your child to name the pictures, then write l under those that end with the same sound as the first picture. **Skill:** Writing l; identifying the final sound l.

ANSWER KEY

NAME

BEGINNING SOUND L

- ladder
- bus
- leaf
- log
- hat
- lamp

Directions: Have your child name the pictures, draw a line from each picture to a square in the lighthouse if the picture name begins with l. *Skill:* Identifying the beginning sound l.

33

NAME

BEGINNING SOUND N

Nn

The Neighbor in the Nest

nest
newspaper
note

34 *Directions:* Have your child look at the picture and say *The Neighbor in the Nest* while listening for the beginning sound. Ask your child to name the items in the picture, then circle those that begin with the same n sound. *Skill:* Identifying the beginning sound n.

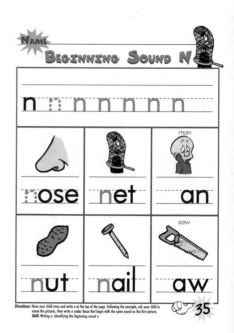

NAME

BEGINNING SOUND N

n n n n n n

- nose
- net
- man / an
- nut
- nail
- saw / aw

Directions: Have your child trace and write n at the top of the page. Following the example, ask your child to name the pictures, then write n under those that begin with the same sound as the first picture. *Skill:* Writing n; identifying the beginning sound n.

35

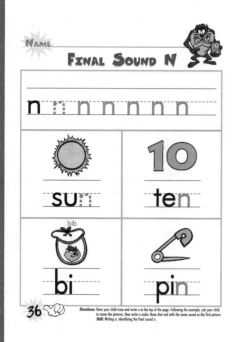

NAME

FINAL SOUND N

n n n n n n

- sun
- ten
- bib / bi
- pin

36 *Directions:* Have your child trace and write n at the top of the page. Following the example, ask your child to name the pictures, then write n under those that end with the same sound as the first picture. *Skill:* Writing n; identifying the final sound n.

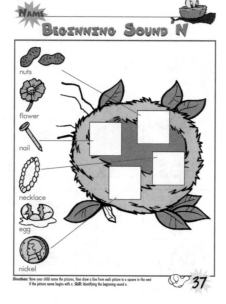

NAME

BEGINNING SOUND N

- nuts
- flower
- nail
- necklace
- egg
- nickel

Directions: Have your child name the pictures, then draw a line from each picture to a square in the nest if the picture name begins with n. *Skill:* Identifying the beginning sound n.

37

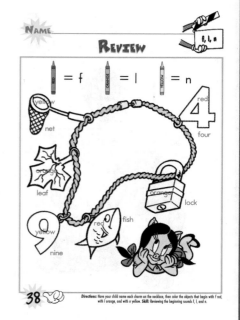

NAME

REVIEW

= f   = l   = n

- net
- leaf
- orange / leaf
- lock
- fish
- red
- four
- nine

Directions: Have your child name each charm on the necklace, then color the objects that begin with f red, with l orange, and with n yellow. *Skill:* Reviewing the beginning sounds f, l, and n.

38

ANSWER KEY

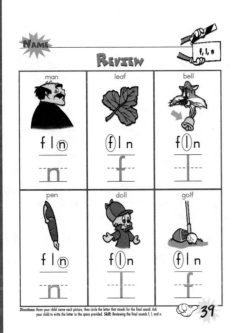

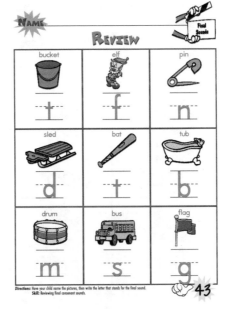

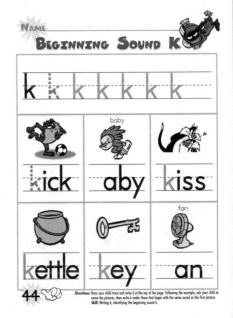

71

ANSWER KEY

FINAL SOUND K

k k k k k k k

hook | book

ring
rin | sneak

Directions: Have your child trace and write *k* at the top of the page. Following the example, ask your child to name the pictures, then write *k* under those that end with the same sound as the first picture.
Skill: Writing *k*; identifying the final sound *k*.

45

BEGINNING SOUND P

p p p p p p p

pie | *table* able | pony

pear | *radio* adio | pail

46

Directions: Have your child trace and write *p* at the top of the page. Following the example, ask your child to name the pictures, then write *p* under those that begin with the same sound as the first picture.
Skill: Writing *p*; identifying the beginning sound *p*.

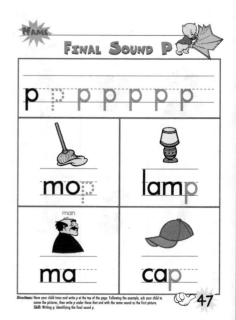

FINAL SOUND P

p p p p p p p

mop | lamp

man
ma | cap

Directions: Have your child trace and write *p* at the top of the page. Following the example, ask your child to name the pictures, then write *p* under those that end with the same sound as the first picture.
Skill: Writing *p*; identifying the final sound *p*.

47

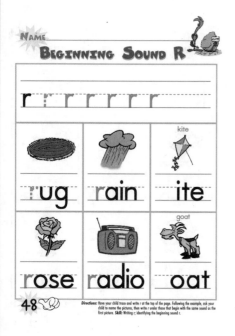

BEGINNING SOUND R

r r r r r r r

rug | rain | *kite* ite

rose | radio | *goat* oat

48

Directions: Have your child trace and write *r* at the top of the page. Following the example, ask your child to name the pictures, then write *r* under those that begin with the same sound as the first picture. *Skill:* Writing *r*; identifying the beginning sound *r*.

FINAL SOUND R

r r r r r r r

sta | *book* boo

4
four | car

Directions: Have your child trace and write *r* at the top of the page. Following the example, ask your child to name the pictures, then write *r* under those that end with the same sound as the first picture.
Skill: Writing *r*; identifying the final sound *r*.

49

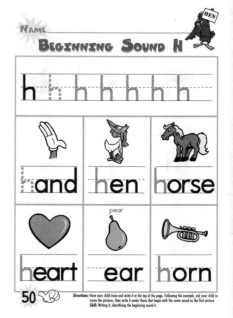

BEGINNING SOUND H

h h h h h h h

hand | hen | horse

heart | *pear* ear | horn

50

Directions: Have your child trace and write *h* at the top of the page. Following the example, ask your child to name the pictures, then write *h* under those that begin with the same sound as the first picture.
Skill: Writing *h*; identifying the beginning sound *h*.

ANSWER KEY

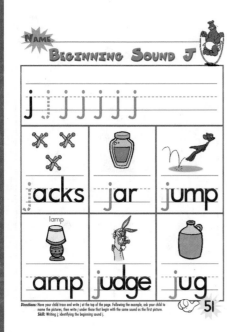

BEGINNING SOUND J

j j j j j j

jacks	jar	jump
lamp		
lamp	judge	jug

Directions: Have your child trace and write j at the top of the page. Following the example, ask your child to name the pictures, then write j under those that begin with the same sound as the first picture.
Skill: Writing j; identifying the beginning sound j.

51

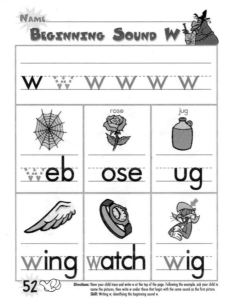

BEGINNING SOUND W

w w w w w w

	rose	jug
web	ose	ug
wing	watch	wig

52

Directions: Have your child trace and write w at the top of the page. Following the example, ask your child to name the pictures, then write w under those that begin with the same sound as the first picture.
Skill: Writing w; identifying the beginning sound w.

REVIEW

hat	jug	well	horn
	jacket		horse
j		h	
jeep	jug	web	hippo
		window	watch
j		w	
harp	juggler	wave	wing
			juice
h	hand	w	

Directions: Have your child name the pictures in each box to find the two with the same beginning sound.
Ask your child to circle the two pictures, then write the letter that stands for the beginning sound.
Skill: Reviewing the beginning sounds h, j and w.

53

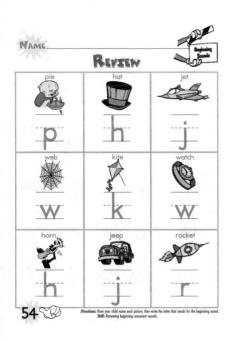

REVIEW

pie	hat	jet
p	h	j
web	kite	watch
w	k	w
horn	jeep	rocket
h	j	r

54

Directions: Have your child name each picture, then write the letter that stands for the beginning sound.
Skill: Reviewing beginning consonant sounds.

BEGINNING SOUND C

c c c c c c

		bird
can	car	ird
	leaf	
comb	eaf	camel

Directions: Have your child trace and write c at the top of the page. Following the example, ask your child to name the pictures, then write c under those that begin with the same sound as the first picture.
Skill: Writing c; identifying the beginning sound c.

55

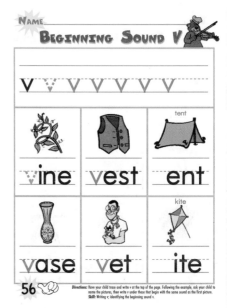

BEGINNING SOUND V

v v v v v v

		tent
vine	vest	ent
		kite
vase	vet	ite

56

Directions: Have your child trace and write v at the top of the page. Following the example, ask your child to name the pictures, then write v under those that begin with the same sound as the first picture.
Skill: Writing v; identifying the beginning sound v.

73

ANSWER KEY

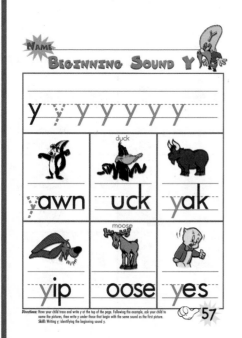

BEGINNING SOUND Y

y y y y y y y

yawn	duck **uck**	yak
yip	moose **oose**	yes

57

BEGINNING SOUND QU

qu qu qu qu

quilt	quiet	seal **eal**
quart	quack	quail

58

BEGINNING SOUND Z

z z z z z z z

zero	zoo	hook **ook**
fish **ish**	zip	dart **art**

59

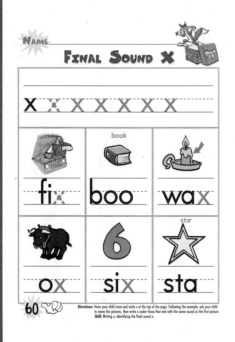

FINAL SOUND X

x x x x x x x

fix	book **boo**	wax
ox	six	star **sta**

60

REVIEW

zigzag	queen
z	qu
zipper	quiet
z	qu
box	six
x	x

61

REVIEW

kite	kangaroo	kettle	tent	king
pig	puppet	ball	pie	pajamas
rooster	goat	rake	radio	raccoon
hat	horn	house	fish	horse
jet	jeep	jar	juggler	lion

62

ANSWER KEY

Offers a selection of workbooks to meet all your needs.

Look for all of these fine educational workbooks
in the McGraw-Hill Learning Materials SPECTRUM Series.
All workbooks meet school curriculum guidelines and correspond to
The McGraw-Hill Companies classroom textbooks.

SPECTRUM SERIES

GEOGRAPHY

Full-color, three-part lessons strengthen geography knowledge and map reading skills. Focusing on five geographic themes including location, place, human/environmental interaction, movement, and regions. Over 150 pages. Glossary of geographical terms and answer key included.

TITLE	ISBN	PRICE
Grade 3, Communities	1-57768-153-3	$7.95
Grade 4, Regions	1-57768-154-1	$7.95
Grade 5, USA	1-57768-155-X	$7.95
Grade 6, World	1-57768-156-8	$7.95

MATH

Features easy-to-follow instructions that give students a clear path to success. This series has comprehensive coverage of the basic skills, helping children to master math fundamentals. Over 150 pages. Answer key included.

TITLE	ISBN	PRICE
Grade 1	1-57768-111-8	$6.95
Grade 2	1-57768-112-6	$6.95
Grade 3	1-57768-113-4	$6.95
Grade 4	1-57768-114-2	$6.95
Grade 5	1-57768-115-0	$6.95
Grade 6	1-57768-116-9	$6.95
Grade 7	1-57768-117-7	$6.95
Grade 8	1-57768-118-5	$6.95

PHONICS

Provides everything children need to build multiple skills in language. Focusing on phonics, structural analysis, and dictionary skills, this series also offers creative ideas for using phonics and word study skills in other language arts. Over 200 pages. Answer key included.

TITLE	ISBN	PRICE
Grade K	1-57768-120-7	$6.95
Grade 1	1-57768-121-5	$6.95
Grade 2	1-57768-122-3	$6.95
Grade 3	1-57768-123-1	$6.95
Grade 4	1-57768-124-X	$6.95
Grade 5	1-57768-125-8	$6.95
Grade 6	1-57768-126-6	$6.95

READING

This full-color series creates an enjoyable reading environment, even for below-average readers. Each book contains captivating content, colorful characters, and compelling illustrations, so children are eager to find out what happens next. Over 150 pages. Answer key included.

TITLE	ISBN	PRICE
Grade K	1-57768-130-4	$6.95
Grade 1	1-57768-131-2	$6.95
Grade 2	1-57768-132-0	$6.95
Grade 3	1-57768-133-9	$6.95
Grade 4	1-57768-134-7	$6.95
Grade 5	1-57768-135-5	$6.95
Grade 6	1-57768-136-3	$6.95

SPELLING

This full-color series links spelling to reading and writing and increases skills in words and meanings, consonant and vowel spellings, and proofreading practice. Over 200 pages. Speller dictionary and answer key included.

TITLE	ISBN	PRICE
Grade 1	1-57768-161-4	$7.95
Grade 2	1-57768-162-2	$7.95
Grade 3	1-57768-163-0	$7.95
Grade 4	1-57768-164-9	$7.95
Grade 5	1-57768-165-7	$7.95
Grade 6	1-57768-166-5	$7.95

WRITING

Lessons focus on creative and expository writing using clearly stated objectives and pre-writing exercises. Eight essential reading skills are applied. Activities include main idea, sequence, comparison, detail, fact and opinion, cause and effect, and making a point. Over 130 pages. Answer key included.

TITLE	ISBN	PRICE
Grade 1	1-57768-141-X	$6.95
Grade 2	1-57768-142-8	$6.95
Grade 3	1-57768-143-6	$6.95
Grade 4	1-57768-144-4	$6.95
Grade 5	1-57768-145-2	$6.95
Grade 6	1-57768-146-0	$6.95
Grade 7	1-57768-147-9	$6.95
Grade 8	1-57768-148-7	$6.95

TEST PREP from the Nation's #1 Testing Company

Prepares children to do their best on current editions of the five major standardized tests. Activities reinforce test-taking skills through examples, tips, practice, and timed exercises. Subjects include reading, math, and language. Over 150 pages. Answer key included.

TITLE	ISBN	PRICE
Grade 3	1-57768-103-7	$8.95
Grade 4	1-57768-104-5	$8.95
Grade 5	1-57768-105-3	$8.95
Grade 6	1-57768-106-1	$8.95
Grade 7	1-57768-107-X	$8.95
Grade 8	1-57768-108-8	$8.95

RECEIVE THE McGRAW-HILL PARENT NEWSLETTER *FREE!*

Thank you for expressing interest in the successful education of your child. With the purchase of this workbook, we know that you are committed to your child's development and future success. We at *McGraw-Hill Learning Materials* would like to help you make a difference in the education of your child by offering a quarterly newsletter that provides current topics on education and activities that you and your child can work on together.

To receive a free copy of our newsletter, please provide us with the following information:

Name _____

Store where
book purchased _____

Address _____   Grade _____

City _____ State ____ Zip _____   Title _____

e-mail (if applicable): _____

The information that you provide will not be given, rented, or sold to any company.

Mail to:
Parent Newsletter
c/o McGraw-Hill Learning Materials
P.O. Box 400
Hilliard, OH 43026-0400

This offer is limited to residents of the United States and Canada and is only in effect for as long as the newletter is published.